Personali

Communicating the Gospel

Angela Butler

Member of the Archbishops' Springboard Team on Evangelism
and Priest in Charge of Chipperfield, Hertfordshire

GROVE BOOKS LIMITED
RIDLEY HALL RD CAMBRIDGE CB3 9HU

Contents

Acknowledgements

I thank God for my colleagues on the Springboard Team: Martin Cavender, Stephen Cottrell and James Lawrence, for their encouragement to develop this work. Thanks also to Bruce Duncan, Sue Jones, Leslie Francis, Janice Price, John Cole and Roger Whitehead whose partnership has helped to further the research and promote the subject.

The Cover Illustration is by Peter Ashton
Copyright © Angela Butler 1999

Church Army and the Grove Evangelism Series

Church Army has over 350 evangelists working in five areas of focus at the cutting edge of evangelism in the UK. It co-sponsors the publication of the Grove Evangelism Series as part of its aim of stimulating discussion about evangelism strategies, and sharing its experience of front-line evangelism.

Further details about Church Army are available from:
Church Army, Independents Road, Blackheath, London SE3 9LG.
Telephone: 0181 318 1226. Fax: 0181 318 5258.
Registered charity number: 226226

First Impression August 1999
ISSN 1367-0840
ISBN 1 85174 411 8

1
Introduction

Have you ever talked to someone about the gospel and found that they just did not seem to *understand* what you were saying? Have you ever disagreed with another Christian about some aspect of your faith only to find that after further discussion you were both saying the same thing?

When starting to work in a parish for the first time I ran a *Saints Alive* course for people enquiring about Christianity. One member of the group continued in my homegroup for another two years and was still not convinced. Then one day my vicar joined the group and we talked about an aspect of the gospel that we had spoken about on many occasions. The 'unconvinced' participant asked the same question that she had asked me over and over again. But when my vicar answered, she suddenly said. 'Now I understand.' Inwardly I raged, 'But that's what I've been saying for two years.' However, it was something to do with the way in which the vicar had put it into words that was different from the way I had expressed it. And of course, it also had to do with God's timing.

Communication can sometimes be a bit like going on holiday to a foreign country where we struggle to make ourselves understood because we do not speak the same language as the person we are talking to. Those same difficulties can occur just as easily when speaking to people in our own language.

It was, therefore, with some excitement that I discovered that using the insights of the Myers Briggs Personality Type Indicator (MBTI®) we can come to understand how to communicate better with people who have a different personality type to ourselves. Through understanding how our personalities affect the ways that we operate and communicate, our relationships with each other can suddenly become a fascinating exercise of trying to speak another person's language.

This understanding can also affect the ways in which we model the gospel and develop as Christians. We know, sometimes to our pain, that differences in personality may manifest themselves to the extent that there is disunity in the church. Worship, services, leadership styles, decision making, can all prove controversial from time to time. Relationships may become strained. Ultimately we need to ask God to teach us in the church how to be united in diversity. Then we can with love allow for each other's preferences.

This booklet is about communicating the gospel. Its aim, therefore, is to help Christians see how God has uniquely gifted them to 'be his witnesses ... to the ends of the earth' (Acts 1.8).

2

A Look at the New Testament

Before we explore the whole question of how personality affects the way we communicate the gospel it may help to set the scene by looking at what we can learn from the Bible on the subject of mission and evangelism.

As Jesus left his disciples he commanded them to 'go and make disciples of all nations, baptizing them in the name of the Father and of the Son and of the Holy Spirit and teaching them to obey everything I have commanded you' (Matt 28.19–20). This commission means that Christ's disciples have a duty to pass on the good news about Jesus. As we look at how Jesus himself evangelized, we notice that in the case of his own disciples:

- he called them to follow him;
- he taught them;
- he sent them.

As we study the progress of the disciples in the gospels one of the questions we may ask is 'at what point did they become Christians?' Was it at the moment they left everything and followed Jesus? Was it somewhere later as they began to absorb Jesus' teaching and to see him preaching and ministering to others? For instance, was it for Peter at the moment he declared 'You are the Christ, the Son of the living God' (Matt 16.16)? Was it for Thomas after the resurrection when he said 'My Lord and my God' (John 20.28)? Or was it a gradual process in which there was no specific point at which they would have said 'now I believe'?

The witness of the New Testament is that for each person it was, and will be, different. Some people may experience conversion as 'crisis'—a discernible event or moment. Others may come to faith over a period of time without a discernible time of 'before' and 'after.' In other words, it is part of a process of conversion or evangelization.

We also see how after Pentecost the early Christians learned to work together, using each other's gifts and skills appropriately. In this we observe that they were concerned to affirm each other's gifts and to work collaboratively in God's service in order to be effective in proclaiming the gospel and serving God.

The New Testament shows us how people, in whatever way they came to faith, continued to develop, learn and change. In other words, the conversion process continued and can be regarded as a lifelong process. Peter spoke to believers about evangelistic witness of good living when he wrote 'Live such good lives among the pagans that … they may see your good deeds and glorify God' (1 Peter 2.12). So the Bible shows us that the gospel is communicated in word and in deed. The more we understand about people, the more effectively we will be able to adapt our evangelistic models and methods to bring the gospel to them.

One of the most striking things we observe in Jesus was his ability to come alongside people as and where they were and lead them on from there. His loving concern for the individual comes through powerfully in the gospels. For instance, he does not condemn the woman caught in adultery, as did the religious leaders looking on, but speaks directly to her condition as both physical and spiritual (John 8.11).

In the case of the disciples we see how, after they are sent out to proclaim the good news, they adapt and develop their evangelistic styles and methods to suit the situation or person they are with. This would have been a challenging time for them because they had no New Testament to help them. The gospel message which they had received and the way in which they communicated it paved the way for many. We see how it was as much through the example of the lifestyle of the believers in Acts 2.42–47 that many joined them. Later on we see Paul debating, reasoning, persuading, and arguing with the Greeks and Jews in Athens by picking up on the gods they had idolized and talking to them about the one true God (Acts 17.16–end).

This section is not complete without noting that threaded through and undergirding the ministry of Jesus and the work of all the believers was an emphasis on prayer. Jesus and the disciples withdrew to pray. They joined in prayer before, during and after preaching, teaching and ministering to people. Through this we learn of their constant reliance on God's Holy Spirit to give them all they needed for the work God had called them to do.

Personality and the Bible

If we are to explore what insights the Bible can give us on personality and communicating the gospel we need to be alert to some possible dangers. Some writers on the subject of the MBTI and spirituality have tried to guess what the personality of key biblical characters might have been. Some have tried to suggest that each gospel has a unique flavour corresponding to each of the four functions in the MBTI personality theory (sensing, intuition, thinking, feeling). But this could tempt us to read into the gospels and gospel characters things which we cannot verify, but only guess at. It risks putting people into boxes rather than receiving the products of their personality through their writings and evidence of their life and work.

Perhaps a better way to approach the subject is to look at how the evidence points to gospel writers using a particular personality preference at a specific time to communicate an aspect of the gospel. We can also look at how, through the stories and examples the gospel writers give us, we can gain insights about preferences used by the people they talk about. These insights may in turn tell us how those people used the personality preferences at particular times to a specific effect in communicating.

For instance, early on in the Bible we see an author demonstrating how the characters he talks about used Extraversion and Introversion co-operatively in God's service. In Exodus 6.28–7.1 Moses, when asked by God to speak to Pharaoh responds 'Since I speak with faltering lips, why would Pharaoh listen to me?' God tells him 'I have made you like God to Pharaoh' and yet God allows Moses to use Aaron as his spokesman. We cannot know for sure what Moses' complaint really was, but how many of us would identify with his words to God? At the end of the day Aaron uses his Extraversion to good effect whilst Moses remains a powerful but perhaps less extravert presence at the meetings with Pharaoh. This may actually say nothing about Moses' preference for Extraversion or Introversion but it does tell us that at the moment they speak to Pharaoh, Aaron was extraverting and Moses was introverting. It is a lovely example of team work and the way that God calls us to co-operate with others in order for his work to be done.

Another example comes from John 8.2 where we see Jesus using silence effectively. Jesus, confronted by the teachers of the law and the Pharisees with a woman caught in adultery is asked a question and fires a conversation-stopping question back. He then lapses into silence. At that moment Jesus employs his Introversion to prompt the crowd to find their own answers. His silence enables them to get in touch with their own thoughts and feelings about his comment—and take his point. Further discussion, further Extraversion, might have been counter-productive.

In this way we can see how biblical writers or authors used their personality preferences to particular effect at particular times without feeling the need to make overall assumptions about their personality type.

3

Some Principles of the MBTI

The MBTI is an extensively researched and well-validated psychometric instrument. It may be administered only by persons who are qualified to use it and it is governed by an ethical code as to the uses to which it may be put. For instance it may not be used as a means of gauging whether someone is suitable for a specific job or a role.

The MBTI is based on a person's *preferences*. The research indicated that everyone is born with certain personality preferences, which they then develop during their lives. Put theologically, personality is a gift from God in creation. And not only that, but just as a child grows and develops, God through his Holy Spirit can help us to develop our personalities throughout our lives. We can choose to co-operate with him or not.

As Christians we aim, through our personalities and other gifts, to become more Christ-like and to produce more of what Paul called the 'fruit of the Spirit'

(Galatians 5.22–23) in our lives—love, joy, peace, patience, kindness, goodness, gentleness, faithfulness and self-control.

Explaining Preference

Personality preferences may be likened to handedness: as children we naturally developed either right-handedness or left-handedness. Whichever hand we write with, using that hand feels more in control than using the other one and so by preference we use that hand. That is not to say that we cannot use the other hand. However, it may require more concentration or feel out of control, awkward or slow until we practise with it. During life we develop not just those parts of personality which come naturally to us but, under God's guidance, we need also to develop those parts of our personality which do not come so naturally.

The following points are necessary to put the MBTI into its proper perspective:

- The MBTI does not fall into the category of psychometric instruments which are classed as tests because it is based on personal *preferences*: it does not measure strengths and weaknesses—it sorts people's preferences. Although scores are given against the preferences expressed in a questionnaire, these indicate only how strongly a person has said they prefer to be this, or that way.
- It is a self-report instrument. A person completes a questionnaire in which they indicate which answers they prefer to certain forced-choice questions.
- Because it is a self-report there are no right or wrong answers.
- A person's answers indicate how they prefer to direct their energy, take in information, make decisions and orient their life.
- The personality type indicator defines 16 personality types.
- It provides the basis for exploration of personality preference, not the final word. That is, it puts people into *growbags*, not boxes!
- It cannot determine whether people will get on with one another.
- All personality types are valuable.
- At the end of the day a person's type can only be verified by themselves.
- It provides *explanations*—not *excuses*.

4

Directing Our Energy:
Extraversion and Introversion

Aren't All Evangelists Extraverts?

Evangelism is often a stumbling block for Christians who do not feel they are Extraverts. Many people's image of the evangelist is that of the extraverted, eloquent, confident speaker. The role of the evangelist is a special one of speaking, or proclaiming, the good news of Jesus Christ and to do this an evangelist has to use his or her Extraversion. All Christians are called to witness and yet the evangelist's role is especially one of speaking out the gospel. But some evangelists have an instinctive preference for Introversion. So what is this all about?

The MBTI speaks of Extraversion as the preference of those whose primary focus of attention is outside themselves. This means that Extraverts (Es) will find their attention naturally drawn towards things outside themselves and this will be where they get their energy from. So, for instance, they will tend to like to be with people and to communicate verbally—this is what will stimulate them and give them energy. Being alone or quiet for too long may be a strain unless they have developed their Introversion well. Es tend to use their speech as a means of processing their thoughts, thus thinking as they are speaking.

Those with a preference for Introversion (Is), however, are those whose primary focus of attention is their inner world of thoughts and feelings. This means that they will be initially drawn to this inner world by preferring to think things through internally before speaking them out. They will tend to get their energy from being alone, or in smaller groups where they have time and space to think before speaking. They may get tired if they spend too much time with other people.

Whether we have a preference for Extraversion or not, we need to use it to communicate. Whether we have a preference for Introversion or not, we need to use it to reflect inwardly. Everybody has both Extraversion and Introversion and will use both in their daily lives. To have a well-balanced personality we need to develop both.

How Extraversion Works in Communicating

Extraversion
Active
Outward
Sociable
People
Many
Expressive
Breadth

What does a preference for **Extraversion** (E) imply for communicating the gospel? Extraverts tend to be attracted, drawn, energized and stimulated by the outer world of people and things. Typically this means that when something sparks off an idea they may speak that thought aloud. They may act before reflecting and may appear to be friendly, talkative and easy to get to know. Because they are energized by their outer world, they tend to need relationships and may express their emotions freely. It is often said of Extraverts that what you see is what you get: their automatic reaction is to tell you what they are thinking or feeling. A preference for Extraversion, however, should not be confused with confidence. Nor does it imply a quality of communication which is better than those with a preference for Introversion.

Whether we are Es or we are communicating the gospel to Es, it is likely that we/they will be comfortable in large groups and will want to talk through issues. Because the Es' instinct is to speak their minds freely, they may enjoy discussion and debate. Sometimes they may appear to think out loud or to interrupt when a thought occurs to them. They may use long or rambling sentences and will probably express their thoughts and feelings quite freely.

Sometimes Es may appear to speak rapidly or rather loudly. They may feel uncomfortable with the Is if they do not express themselves or respond in discussion. They may feel threatened by too much silence. Because they tend to prefer verbal communication they may like to listen to tapes or videos about the gospel and talk about them afterwards. Their search, initially, may be for the extraverted God—the God who is out there, energizing and involved in the world.

How Introversion Works in Communicating

Introversion
Reflective
Inward
Reserved
Privacy
Few
Quiet
Depth

Those with a preference for **Introversion** (**I**), are those whose primary focus of attention is inside themselves. These people tend to be stimulated, drawn and energized by their inner world of thoughts, reflections and experiences. This means that they are likely to think something through internally before they speak or act. As a result they may prefer written communication which gives them time to think and consider. They may appear to be more reserved or harder to get to know. They may share their feelings only with a selected few. They may bottle up thoughts and feelings or need a degree of space or quiet. If the Is do not use their balancing Extraversion enough they may become withdrawn or inexpressive.

In terms of communicating the gospel this means that the Is are likely to be more comfortable with small groups or one-to-one discussion. If they have developed their Extraversion well, they may be happy with large groups if they can feel anonymous within them or if they do not have to contribute unless they wish. I remember a new enquirers' course in which, applying my best 'meeting technique,' I asked someone who had said nothing all evening what she thought about the topic being discussed. She froze in horror at being put on the spot and never came to another session.

I am now much more sensitive to people's need to exercise their Introversion until they feel comfortable about talking. I may sometimes allow them to remain silent for several sessions (whilst also checking with them when no-one else is around). That is not to say that I would encourage non-participation or laziness in group discussion, but would try to seek God's timing about when to encourage them gently to contribute. When speaking to people we often imagine that we have to keep the conversation going and we can become uncomfortable with silence because we assume that communication is flawed unless words flow. Balance is the key.

Because the Is often prefer to read about a subject before (and after) discussing it, good books or pamphlets may help them in their search for facts and the truth of the gospel. We should not be put off if they pause before speaking or responding to a question. Sometimes they may need that space and silence, particularly in the middle of a busy day, and may be put off if some people talk too much. Their search for God may be expressed or experienced as a search for the God within—the still, small voice.

It is, therefore, good to build some God-given silence into our programmes, groups, worship and contact times so that the Is can get in touch with their thoughts and feelings. We can do this by simply providing some silence at various points. For instance, we can allow two to three minutes of silence after sermons, talks or readings before we launch into discussion or the next item in the programme. We can set aside silent and talking areas in places where we meet and give people permission to exercise their preferences without feeling embarrassed. I have often created space, sometimes with music in the background, and made people work alone on something before discussing in small groups afterwards.

Similarly when working in a team, for instance on missions, it is important to allow team members to mirror their preferences in the way they work. Some can keep extraverting all day whereas others need time to re-energize using their Introversion without feeling unsociable. It all points to the need to work co-operatively in teams so that we affirm the way that God has created us while helping one another express that uniqueness to maximum effectiveness as we serve God in communicating the gospel.

5

Collecting Information in Life:
Sensing and Intuition

You Have Got to Give People the Facts!

At the end of the first session of an Alpha course a participant asked for material to read at home during the week. We suggested he read the Gospel of Matthew. The next week he came back with 'a serious problem' for us. Having read the genealogy at the beginning of Matthew he remembered seeing another in Luke. He then started to compare the two genealogies side-by-side on his computer. As he did so he realized that there was a gap of 200 years in the middle of one of them which was proving to be a major stumbling block to belief.

We knew immediately that this participant was in search of detailed facts. We noticed, however, that other participants were quickly bored by long detailed explanations about faith or doctrinal issues. They wanted to look more at the bigger picture—the vision. Their questions were aimed to ask 'what possibilities does this open up?'

The MBTI research revealed that people collect their information in life, on which they subsequently base their decisions, using one of two 'Perceiving' functions. Either **Sensing (S)**—collecting information using the five senses or **iNtuition (N)**—collecting information using the so-called sixth sense. All of us have both functions but we tend to prefer one above the other and so will use that one first.

How the Sensing Function Works in Communicating

Sensing
Facts
Details
Practical
Literal
Sequential
Simple
Clear
Present
Down to earth

People with a preference for the **Sensing (S)** perception will instinctively focus on facts and details which they can experience through the five senses of sight, sound, touch, taste, smell. They may ask precise questions and be looking for precise answers. They may like a step-by-step explanation or progression of thought and they are likely to be looking for a down-to-earth faith which is concrete and practical.

It will be important to impress upon the Ss the historical aspects of the gospel; to show how them how it makes sense and how Christianity can be lived out in daily life. These people may be helped by an experience of God through their senses—beauty, music, smell and taste. Because of this their focus tends to be on the *present* moment, on what is coming to these senses *now*. Sometimes we can pick up that someone has a preference for Sensing because they tend to ask the 'what' and 'how' questions.

A biblical occasion in which we see a preference for Sensing being exercised is in the example of when Thomas was not prepared to believe that Jesus had risen from the dead until he had *seen* and *touched* him (John 20.25). Jesus lovingly respects Thomas's personality and allows him to do just that. However, Jesus then challenges him to 'stop doubting and believe.' Faced with such evidence Thomas's reaction was the heartfelt 'My Lord and my God.'

How the iNtuition Function Works in Communicating

iNtuition
Abstract
Theoretical
Conceptual
Imprecise
Visionary
Hunches
Patterns
Future

Those who have a preference for **iNtuitive (N)** perception, however, are likely to be interested in hearing a fresh or unique message. Their focus tends to be on the future and possibilities—towards what might be. They may, therefore, be interested in the future implications of belief and faith and the possibilities which it opens up.

Ns seem to have an ability to collect information through metaphor, implication, symbolism and poetry. They are sometimes seen to have leap-frog minds because of their ability to make sudden connections. They often like to see the 'big picture' or 'wider vision' and can be moved by symbols in language and sight.

When speaking to **N**s we may find they tend to use more general terms and may sometimes be identified through their asking of the 'why' questions. They may want to adapt their message to a person's needs and concerns and inspire people to take the risk of faith. Making connections through mapping their journey to faith may help them to see where God has been in their lives.

The use of symbols needs to be different for **S**s and **N**s. For instance, the **S**s may need some understanding or explanation of the symbol before it can mean anything to them and they can move on with it. However, if a symbol is explained too much to the **N**s it may lose its power for them and become irrelevant.

In recent times the use of the creative arts to communicate the gospel has grown. This seems to be particularly effective where symbol, art, dance, drama/mime, poetry, music, banners and so on are used to illustrate, support or complement a gospel message. Sometimes people seem to experience God through their Sensing or iNtuition in these art forms in a way which is more powerful than words. Pictures used on an OHP or picture cards handed out have been successful in leading people to a new experience of God during a wordless meditation.

The Gospel of John contains many concepts, images and visionary language which suggest that the writer often used iNtuition to convey his message. For instance, 'In the beginning was the Word and the Word was with God' (John 1.1); 'I am the bread of life' (John 6.35); 'I am the vine' (John 15.1). These passages suggest that the writer was using, or recording, iNtuitive phrases to convey his meaning. The phrases are full of possibilities and meaning, leaving the door open to further insights and inspiration. John's gospel is at times enigmatic and poetic as if the writer thought it unimportant to spell out the details of his meaning or message but wanted to leave it as an invitation to the iNtuition of others. The prophets also sometimes demonstrate the use of iNtuition in the way that their futuristic, visionary pronouncements spelt out to the people the consequences of their behaviour, calling them back to the ever-faithful God of Israel.

6
Making Decisions in Life: Thinking and Feeling

How Do I Know It Is True?

Some years ago, a straw poll at a MBTI workshop at which there were an equal number of people with a preference for Thinking and Feeling demonstrated the differences well. When asked the question 'What would you say it was that meant most to you when you registered belief for the first time?' the Thinkers replied 'Well, it was true' and the Feelers replied 'I had an experience of God's love.'

Having collected our information in life using the perceiving functions, Sensing or iNtuition, the research showed that people then use that information to make decisions using two 'Judging' functions—Thinking and Feeling. Both ways of making decisions are rational but start from a different perspective. People have, and need to use, both functions when making decisions.

How the Thinking Function Works in Communicating

Thinking
Logical
Objective
Coherent
Analyse
Principled
Competent
Profound

People with a preference for **Thinking** (T) judgment tend to like a logical analysis of issues and to work through the logical implications. They may appear to 'test' others or their knowledge—especially if that person is the leader of a group or an evangelist. Sometimes we may find the Ts wanting to engage in reasoning which seems like arguing but is actually a genuine attempt to get to the truth of an issue. This is not necessarily meant to challenge a leader and may just be an expression of their desire to find the truth. Their tendency is to want to take a long objective look at the evidence and apply just and impartial judgment to it. They may therefore appear to weigh objective evidence and may seem to be intellectual or cool as they decide using their heads.

The Ts may not initially be impressed by faith stories or other people's testimonies/examples. However, it is said that they may be influenced by an appeal to trust in the faith of others if they respect the integrity of the other person. Initially it may be difficult for them to understand the concept of a personal God or the need for a relationship with God. I remember well someone who, hearing an evangelistic talk at a men's breakfast, was completely turned-off by the speaker's insistence that everyone 'needs a personal relationship with Jesus.' This is something that the Ts may need more time to understand and get in touch with.

Bible study may be very helpful for the T's faith development and in time they may come to regard it as a form of prayer for them. Their questions may revolve around such things as evidence, historicity and purpose. Their faith interests may be seen or worked out in areas to do with justice and righteousness in terms of the issue, the policy, the law and so on rather than ministry to the people affected by it. Finally, they may need the reassurance that faith is not blind belief but, to have integrity, it must necessarily involve struggle and intellectual questioning.

We find examples of the use of Thinking in the Bible in the Gospel of Matthew. Matthew, coming from a Judaistic, legalistic background sets out to prove in his opening chapter in a logical, analytical way, that Jesus was the prophesied Messiah in the line of David. He focuses on showing how, in Jesus, all righteousness is fulfilled by justifying, in legalistic terms, the actions of Jesus.

Another example of the use of the Thinking function is in Paul's letter to the Romans chapter 8. Here Paul appears to use Thinking with iNtuition to wrestle with and analyse theological concepts and reach conclusions. The result is a powerful theological treatise which will thrill some but require enormous concentration for others.

How the Feeling Function Works in Communicating

Feeling
Personal
Subjective
Values
Harmony
Tactful
Helpful
Persuasive
People

Those with a preference for **Feeling** (**F**) judgment, in contrast, may need to feel a rapport with or to trust those who speak to them about faith. For them the personal relationship—both with others and with God—may play a strong influential role. Because they tend to decide with 'the heart' on the basis of their moral and ethical values they may be influenced by how faith or belief will meet theirs and other people's needs. They may look for harmony, reconciliation and peace and may talk a lot about the impact of moral issues on people's lives.

Unlike the **T**s, the **F**s are likely to be interested in other people's faith stories and testimonies. They are also likely to be interested in social action to do with people and so their questions may well focus on things like suffering and other religions.

Sometimes we may find that **F**s are carrying past hurts or grievances towards the church or towards Christians which have become stumbling blocks to faith or fellowship. In these cases it is unlikely that logic on its own will heal the memories but relationships with loving Christians might enable them to move forward again.

A biblical example of the use of the Feeling function is when Jesus meets with the 'sinful woman' who anoints him with perfume (Matt 26.8). Here he shows his use of Feeling judgment in response to her very demonstrative display of care when she pours her jar of expensive perfume over his feet. She shows concern for his bodily needs and he commends her for her *love*. Jesus rebukes those who accuse her of extravagant waste. In telling her that her sins are forgiven he makes personal his reply to her. She must have felt his personal care for *her*.

Luke in his gospel shows a particular interest in people or stories about people which are not included in the other gospels. For instance, Luke includes the stories about the prodigal son, the good samaritan, the pharisee and the publican. All these stories can be used to powerfully convey God's unconditional love to people to whom we want to communicate the gospel. At other times Luke focuses on people and their reactions, responses, and feelings and brings us insights into the characters of people. In bringing us the songs of Mary and Zechariah in a loving and descriptive way he beautifully conveys the joy, excitement and praise of these characters and brings them alive to us.

The following table summarizes the above information.

When talking to, explaining to, preaching to or trying to understand, bear in mind the following aspects for each personality function:

Sensing	iNtuition
Give a step by step presentation	Give the big picture
Be factual	Talk in general terms
Give details	Point out future benefits/opportunities
Be concise	Be confident and enthusiastic
Keep it simple and down to earth	Indicate challenges
Show why it makes sense	Be creative and imaginative
Demonstrate practical applications to life	Be visionary
Give historical perspective	Be conceptual, using doctrines, symbols etc
Give examples of how it has worked in the past: peopleÕs lives, history of the Church, contribution to world issues etc	Talk about possibilities
	Try to make the message sound fresh or unique.
Aim: To show how the gospel is historically based, makes sense, and how it is to be lived out in daily life.	Aim: To adapt the way we present the message to a persons needs and concerns. To be a catalyst, and inspire others to take the risk of faith.
Thinking	Feeling
Be logical	Be friendly and personable
Give objective evidence	Make it personal
Well-organized	Show implications for peopleÕs lives
Indicate the principles involved	Indicate how it will help
Emphasize truth and authenticity	Talk about Gospel values
Engage in intellectual debate/discussion	Be warm and sympathetic
Be competent/assured	Be tactful
Be prepared to be ÔtestedÕ or questioned	Be prepared to answer questions about how it affects others
Talk about the pros and cons	Use personal testimonies
Aim: To show the truth, justice and authenticity of the gospel. Faith is not blind belief but, to have integrity, it must necessarily involve struggle and intellectual questioning.	Aim: To show how the gospel is a message of love that demands a heart-felt response of self-giving love to our Lord and Saviour.

(The above aims are taken from a handout by the Rev'd Canon Bruce Duncan, Principal of Sarum College, and are used with his permission.)

7
Orientating Our Lives: Judgment and Perception

Make-Up-Our-Mind Time?

The last two aspects of the MBTI refer to a so-called fourth dimension which relates to the way that people like to run, or orientate, their lives—their attitude towards the outer world. These two attitudes are named Judgment and Perception.

How Judgment Works in Communicating

Judgment
Organized
Planned
Structure
Control
Decisive
Deliberate
Closure
Productive

It was found in the research that those who prefer to use a **Judgment** (J) process to run their outer world have a natural drive to want to have things decided, judged, settled, planned, organized and managed according to a plan. This is described as the judging attitude toward the outer world.

When communicating the gospel this means that for Js, decision making or choosing is likely to be their goal and their goal for others. They may see this as 'getting a result,' a conversion or whatever. They may structure their talks or events in ways which will seek to bring things to a head—to trigger a conclusion or a response. They may become impatient with signs of lack of decision or of progress. The evangelistic event with an invitation to come forward and 'give your life to Jesus today' is typical of a J approach.

In general, Js like things to be orderly. They like to have a sense of being under control and they may get frustrated by lengthy, wandering discussions which appear to be going nowhere. For this reason they may be attracted by well-organized activities which stick to time. They may be put off by what they see as sloppy or unclear structures, events or worship. They may experience stress or produce adverse reactions if they feel that things are out of control. Their inclination is to reflect in their lives and teaching the God who brings order out of chaos. We may sometimes recognize them from their use of the '...ed' words—such as looked, compared, assessed.

When Peter preached on the day of Pentecost he finished by pleading with the crowd to 'save yourselves from this corrupt generation' (Acts 2.40). Here Peter appears to use a J process to bring people to a point of decision. It is clearly effective as we are told that about three thousand responded. Furthermore, Peter presented his hearers with a positive way of responding 'repent and be baptized' (Acts 2.38).

In a different context in 1 Timothy, Paul's J attitude seems to be trying to urge order and structure in the lives of prominent Christians and in the conduct of church business. Paul appears to use Thinking judgment as he presents to his hearers a logical, orderly, managed structure for the conduct of the church.

How Perception Works in Communicating

Perception
Flexible
Flow
Experience
Curious
Spontaneous
Openness
Receptive
Adapt

Others, however, prefer to use a **Perception (P)** process to run their outer life. These people have a natural drive towards keeping things open. They tend to want to remain flexible so as to adapt to changing circumstances and to experience life as widely as possible. They enjoy processing. They may be less concerned about reaching decisions because they enjoy using their perceiving functions (**S** and **N**) in the outward mode to process information.

When communicating the gospel to **P**s we may find they are naturally curious. As a result they may follow leads and go with the flow of life or of conversation easily. They may delay making decisions but when they do, they may do so in a rush or change their minds afterwards.

Years ago a young seeker 'gave her life to Christ' during a very moving time of prayer at the end of an enquirers' course. In the following three years she made two further commitments. Each occasion I said to her 'but I thought you did that *x* years ago?' Her reply each time was 'this is different.' Each time, I wondered what had happened on the previous occasions. It appeared that for her each decision was not necessarily the final one.

When I spoke to another **P** about his experience of conversion he spoke of two occasions when he had made a commitment. The second, he said, was not *ex nihilo* (out of nothing) but was made in the light of a *deeper* understanding and commitment than the first. This suggests that for some **P**s conversion may come in different stages. Perhaps it is a process of developing and refining belief which is not experienced as so decisive as that for **J**s. As a result **P**s may express the latest commitment as if it were 'real' for the first time.

To a **J** it may seem that those who use a **P** process to run their outer life spend time on options and information and want to remain open-minded for as long as possible. **P**s may bring up many interesting issues, whether they are relevant or not, and they may be put off by programmes or schedules which restrict their ability to explore without limits. Whether leading or participating, they may not always be good time keepers. They may become so absorbed in what they are doing that they forget the time. We may recognize them from their use of the '...ing' words—looking, comparing, exploring.

We see examples in the Bible of the **P** process governing people's behaviour when they responded in certain ways to God's Holy Spirit. There were, it seems, occasions when they became very open, adaptable and spontaneous. Through their willingness to go wherever, whenever, we may see an increased ability in people to use their perceptive process to run their outer life.

It might be tempting to think that the Holy Spirit is all about Perception and yet we see Paul arguing in 1 Corinthians 14 that a spirit-led fellowship needs the balancing '**J**'—order and discipline. Here Paul appears to employ a **J** attitude to persuade the Corinthians to bring some order to a situation in which there appears to have been too much Perception in operation—too much 'going with the flow.'

In reverse, in another situation in Athens (Acts 17.16–32). Paul goes around the city employing a **P** attitude to observe the religious idols the Athenians had erected. The opening of Paul's speech to them shows flexibility and an openness to the Athenian culture but he then uses a **J** process to channel their thoughts towards his message. His speech leads them to a point where some felt able to decide.

8

An Impossible Task?

We may at this point think that it is an impossible task to cater for all personality types when communicating the gospel, but we can take some simple steps.

Firstly, we can adopt a listening attitude. If we do this we will pick up pieces of information from people which may suggest their personality preferences. We can then try to meet them, initially on their own ground, and lead them on from there.

Secondly, if we have time to prepare, we can look at how we can include something for each of the four functions (Sensing, iNtuition, Thinking and Feeling). For instance we can try to include some aspect of *all* of the following in events or talks.

For those with a preference for:
Sensing: Something concrete and practical.
iNtuition: Something of vision.
Thinking: Something of understanding.
Feeling: Some silence.

Thirdly, we can help each other by sharing our personality gifts. In the teams I have worked in I have learned to recognize and appreciate the different personalities of those around me. For instance when I, as an **S** (Sensing), need new ideas or something creative to communicate the gospel I turn to my iNtuition preferring colleagues who are usually full of creative ideas. Where my instinct is to use things which have worked well for me in the past they are able to encourage me to take the risk of doing something differently. When my Thinking preferring colleagues want to assess the impact on people of something they want to say they may consult me, an **F**. By working together in this way we can aim provide something for everyone—however small.

9

A God of Surprises?

Although we can learn a great deal about behaviour and personality with the help of the MBTI at the end of the day God overrules. This section looks at how God sometimes turns things upside down when dealing with us through our personalities.

A further aspect to the MBTI theory relates to the order in which it found that people use the four functions: Sensing, iNtuition, Thinking and Feeling. It was found that people will use these in a particular order according to their personality type. This means that they have a tendency to use their functions in a predictable order of 1-2-3-4.

The logic of this is likened to the hierarchy on a ship: Someone needs to be the captain and others need to act in support according to rank rather than to compete for control of the ship. The hierarchy of these functions was named:

1. Dominant function   4. Inferior or Shadow function
2. Auxiliary function ———→ 3. Tertiary function

The above demonstrates the theory that the most preferred function (1, or dominant function) is always opposite to the least preferred function (4, inferior or shadow function). And the auxiliary function (2) is always opposite to the tertiary function (3).

In addition it was found that if a Perceptive process (Sensing or iNtuition) is dominant then a Judging process (Thinking or Feeling) will act in support of it. This means that if a perceptive process (**S** or **N**) is dominant, the Judging processes (**T** and **F**) will be the auxiliary (2) and tertiary (3) and vice versa. This creates balance so that a Perceiving process is supported by a Judging process. The following examples demonstrate the order and balance of the four functions:

If my most preferred functions are: *Then my least preferred function will be:*
1. Sensing perception (S)   4. iNtuitive perception (N)
2. Thinking judgment (T)   3. Feeling judgment (F)

The above shows how if my dominant function is Sensing then my shadow function will be iNtuition and vice versa (Perceiving functions). In order to create balance the auxiliary and tertiary functions are Judging functions (Thinking and Feeling).

If my most preferred functions are: *Then my least preferred function will be:*
1. Feeling judgment (F)   4. Thinking judgment (T)
2. iNtuitive perception (N)   3. Sensing perception (S)

The above shows how if my dominant function is Feeling then my shadow function will be Thinking and vice versa (Judging functions). In order to create balance the auxiliary and tertiary functions are Perceiving functions (iNtuition and Sensing).

For the final parts of the equation it was found that if a person used their dominant process mainly in the outer world of people and things, that person's orientation was called Extraverted. If they used it mainly in the world of inner thoughts and ideas it was called Introverted. In other words, the Dominant function may be Extraverted or Introverted according to a person's preference.

Lastly the so-called J–P scale tells us which function people extraverted. So if, for instance, they came out a J, then they would extravert either their Thinking or Feeling (and Introvert the other functions). If they came out a P then they would extravert either their Sensing or iNtuition (and extravert their other functions).

The following gives some examples of how this applies to four of the personality types:

ISTJ	ENFP	ISFP	ENTJ
1. Dominant S (I)	1. Dominant N (E)	1. Dominant F (I)	1. Dominant T (E)
2. Auxiliary T (E)	2. Auxiliary F (I)	2. Auxiliary S (E)	2. Auxiliary N (I)
3. Tertiary F (E)	3. Tertiary T (I)	3. Tertiary N (E)	3. Tertiary S (I)
4. Inferior N (E)	4. Inferior S (I)	4. Inferior T (E)	4. Inferior F (I)

The letters in brackets indicate the direction of the function; that is, (E) means that it is extraverted, (I) means that it is introverted.

Since the purpose of this booklet is to alert to us to differences in personality and not to teach a complete MBTI theory, we do not need to know a person's dominant and shadow functions when communicating the gospel. What is important to register is that research showed that because we have *most* control over our dominant function we have *decreasing* control over the other ones. We therefore have *least* control over our shadow function.

It is, therefore, interesting that sometimes people report that it was apparently through their shadow function that they have had some spontaneous experience of God. Similarly it appears that sometimes God may use the shadow function to convert someone because he or she has least control over it.

Translated, this means, for instance, that we could hear someone asking us for facts and details with their dominant Sensing function but God may convince or surprise them through a concept, a symbol or a vision out of their shadow—iNtuition. Or we may hear someone asking us for concepts and theories with their dominant iNtuition but God may convince or surprise them through some tiny detail or fact or some revelation of himself through sight, sound, taste, smell or touch coming from their shadow—Sensing.

The person with a dominant preference for Thinking may be seeking the truth and suddenly find themselves touched or influenced by the love of God or by a people issue out of their shadow—Feeling. The person with a dominant preference for Feeling may be seeking a personal relationship with God and find God challenging them to face the truth in a logical analytical way through their shadow—Thinking, which gives them some sudden deep insight or understanding.

When people have an experience of God through their inferior, or shadow function, it may take them by surprise and make them feel overwhelmed or awed by the experience. They may react or behave in what onlookers would regard as an uncharacteristic way. So long as we are satisfied that this experience *is* from God, we may be able to encourage them to respond to God in ways which they might not normally consider 'their way.'

Ultimately God wants us to open the whole of our personalities to him. With his guidance we can develop the parts we least prefer throughout life. Maturity in personality terms is the capability to use whatever process is needed when it is most needed. This means that we will need to co-operate with God in developing ourselves, and encouraging others to develop those processes we/they find hard or awkward to use.

Following are a couple of biblical examples of the way that the shadow function may have featured. First is the story of the rich young man's encounter with Jesus (Matt 19.16). The rich young man asks Jesus, '*What* good thing must I *do* to get eternal life?' (Present, specific, practical—Sensing?—give-away words in italics). Jesus then appears to use his Sensing by giving him a list of things he can do. Then after the man's reply that he has kept this list of commandments Jesus switches and tells him to 'sell all your possessions and give to the poor and you will have treasure in heaven. Then come, follow me' (Matt 19.21).

For the rich young man the concept of treasure in heaven and the implications of future possibilities over which he would have no control (iNtuition and Perception) were so unfamiliar and uncomfortable that he was not prepared to risk it. One wonders whether they were coming out of his shadow function which he might have felt 'scary' and less able to control. If this were so it could have produced within him a negative reaction which meant that he was not, at that moment, able to cope with Jesus' invitation to journey into new territory both materially and spiritually.

The other example of a conversion experience is that of Saul on the road to Damascus. Many of Paul's writings lead us to believe that he might have had a preference for Thinking. Yet at the moment of conversion what seems to hit him are in the words from the voice from heaven 'Saul, Saul, why are you persecuting *me*.' Part of Saul's post-conversion wrestling was to do with the realization that he had not just been persecuting a religion or sect but a *person*.

Did God at this moment use Saul's shadow function, Feeling, to catapult him into confronting his actions and his beliefs and bringing him face to face with the person of God in Jesus Christ?

At the moment of conversion, or at stages in life when God moves us on in our journey with him, we may experience God's refining hand reaching towards us through the less preferred parts of our personality. Our giving in to him with our whole being is what he longs for and this is why conversion can be referred to as a lifelong process.

10
God's Perspectives

An understanding of the theory of the MBTI does not mean that, because we might be able to work out what information people need or how people might behave, we can be tempted to rely less on God. At the end of the day communicating the gospel and conversion are the work of the Holy Spirit. It is our privilege and joy to be used by God in his mission to the world.

We need to be constantly calling upon God to give us the discernment and flexibility to work with him in meeting people's needs and bringing them to a living faith. We can only try to co-operate with God more fully as we come alongside people. This starts with respecting the way that God has made each person and trying to follow Jesus' example of coming alongside them and starting where they are.

At all times we need to remember that since faith is a journey, we are called to help people along the road. We may, therefore, be sowers and not reapers in the spiritual harvest. If we can rejoice in the little God asks us to do then we may be released from any burden or belief that we are solely responsible for the conversion of the world—today!

Many has been the occasion when over the years I have made assumptions about people's faith or lack of faith only to be proved wrong. God has taught me that his infinite variety of ways of reaching and touching people is endless. I need to beware of boxing him or assuming that there are particular ways of preaching, teaching or evangelizing. God is always bigger than we imagine but with the help of an understanding of personality we can help others to experience him in a greater variety of ways.

We also need to remember to work at how we co-operate with God by co-operating with one another. In recent years it has been an enormous joy for me to experience the variety of ways we can communicate the gospel with the aid of different personalities, gifts and traditions. This *does* require a great deal of humility and openness to how God can work through people who are different from ourselves or in ways which are very different from our preferences. But we are called to model unity in diversity and to discern how God may want us to adapt our communication to meet the needs of our age.

At the end of the day we can all rejoice in the knowledge that God has made us and loves us. He makes us as unique beings. We respond to him in our own unique way. Through our prayer and worship and lives we serve him and speak about him in our own unique way. This is a cause for rejoicing, not despair. This is to be encouraged and not stifled.

I pray that this booklet will encourage every Christian to discover more fully how they may 'declare the praises of him who called you out of darkness into his wonderful light' (1 Peter 2.9).

Bibliography

I'm not crazy, I'm just not you by Roger R Pearman and Sarah C Albritton (Davies Black Publishing, 1997)

Prayer and Temperament by Chester P Michael and Marie C Norrisey (Open Door Inc, 1984)

Effective Teaching, Effective Learning by Alice and Lisa Fairhurst (Davies Black Publishing, 1995)

Gifts Differing by Isabel Myers Briggs (Consulting Psychologists' Press, 1992)

Using Type in Selling by Susan A Brock (Consulting Psychologists' Press, 1994)

Pray Your Way by Bruce Duncan (Darton, Longman and Todd, 1994)

Tell It With Style by Helen T Boursier (Inter-Varsity Press, 1995)